Contents

Why Read Poetry?.. 6
Meditation 8
Seeking God 10
It Just Is 12
This Killin' Thing 13
Star Dust.. 14
Me 17
Meditation Mantra 19
The Poor 20
Letting Go 22
One Thing 24
Incarnations 25
Thank You Universe 28
Relativity 30
Creating Reality 30
At 4 Years Old 31
Losing One's Life To Save It 32
Your Body 34
Islands 35
The Moon 36
At Least For Today 36
A Father's Love 37
Being 39

Body Surfing	40
Breathe	41
Evolution	43
Why Are We Here?	46
Ode to Martha Jean	48
Pam	52
Just Be	55
Ants	56
Growing Old	58
The Death of a Loved One	59
Arguing With My Best Friend	61
Frustration	63
I Am Life	64
Two Worlds	65
The Real Jesus	66
A Perfect Moment	70
The Music	72
The Singer	74
An Old Man's Brain	75
Dying	77
The Bible	78
Secular and Sacred	80
Imperfection	81
The Preacher	83

Mother Teresa of Calcutta 86
Anger 87
"Unless You Become Like a Little Child" 88
A Modern Translation of Matthew 5:3-12 89
Ode to Gary Calvin 90
My Dilemma 93
If I Could Travel Back in Time 95
The Enemy 97
Tree of Life 99
To My Mother 101
Love Is 103
Leaving Assisi 105
Gratitude & Trust 107
The Big Picture 109
Love, Laugh and Let Go 111
Staring at a Full Moon Over the Ocean at Night with Erwin Schrodinger 112
Healing the Subconscious 114

Why Read Poetry?

Like good music,
Good poems often take you
Where prose cannot.

We know so little
About the universe
And ourselves;
But occasionally
We get glimpses of truth.

Some of the most profound truths
Can only be expressed in poetry.
Sometimes, poems can say in a few lines
What entire books fail to say.

Poems reveal blind spots
And contradictions.
They challenge long held ideas
That no longer ring true.
They remind us
There is always more to the story.

Poems stir emotions.
They help us get out of our heads
And into our hearts

Where deeper truths hide.

Poems heal.
They reveal connections
In a world full of disconnections.
They help us let go
Of past disappointments,
And live more fully
In the present.

Poems are like life.
Full of mysteries
And miracles.

Don't rush them.
Give them your full attention.

The Universe speaks most clearly
Through a poem.
Perhaps the Universe
Is a poem.

Meditation

The human animal
Is a vast ocean.
He spends most his time
Rising, rolling and falling along the surface;
Interacting
With the sun, the wind and the storms;
Providing food
For sea gulls and fisherman.

The surface is often
Beautiful and tranquil,
Strengthening one's faith
In a benevolent creator.

But then,
Driven by universal forces
Beyond his control,
His random and ever-moving waves of emotion and thought
Sometimes grow into large swells and surges,
Sinking ships, eroding beaches and washing away villages.

Occasioned by pain, boredom or sense of adventure,
He might momentarily find himself
In the depths of the sea
Where cold darkness and sea monsters
Threaten his very soul.
The mysteries and contradictions
Of this infinite deepness
Cause him to question

His familiar and predictable surface,
Where myths of mighty heroes and far off kingdoms
Once gave him a shallow sense of security,
At least on sunny days.

He usually finds a way back to the surface,
Avoiding Titanic's fate.
Sometimes his thoughts and emotions
Become more liberal,
Trying to accommodate
The much larger universe
Briefly experienced beneath the surface.

Occasionally, this brave heart may return
To the depths,
Driven by glimpses of sunken treasure
Or long forgotten pirate tales
Suddenly remembered.
He may even learn
To breathe underwater
Like a beautiful mermaid.

Then he will visit often
And stay long,
But he must always return
To the surface
Where his body is meant to dwell,
Until death returns him
To the great depths
Wherein he was born;
To finally swim eternally
In the great ocean of pure Being.

Seeking God

Seeking God
Is like a fish
Swimming through the ocean
Looking for the ocean.

Seeking God
Is like a bird
Soaring through the air
Looking for the air.

Seeking God
Is like a man with amnesia
Looking for himself.

Everything is ultimately one thing.
Separated in 4 dimensions,
But not in 5.

It all just is.
And it's good,
Because being
Trumps non-being.

So just be.
One of a zillion
Life forms,
Resisting pain and
Seeking pleasure.

Evolving,
And learning,

Slowly,
That "we all do better, when we all do better."

Evolving
And hoping,
Cautiously,
That the Universe is intelligent
And loving.

Evolving
And seeing,
Occasionally,
That we are the Universe
Remembering,
Moment by moment,
Its history.

It Just Is

It just is - the good and the bad.

It just is.

The pain, the blindness, the selfishness makes me sad.

But it just is.

Will it get better?
Will evolution finally put pain asunder?

Maybe, maybe not

I hope, I wonder.

Pain may be the canvas
Upon which the universe paints a beautiful picture.
Pain makes pleasure all the more richer.

Can pleasure exist without pain?
Does wrong give meaning to right?
In the beginning darkness was everywhere,
Then God said, "Let there be light."
Can light exist without darkness?

We know so little, but this is plain:
We embrace the pleasure and resist the pain.

Can my flesh cry out with your pain?
Can your heart rejoice with my good fortune?
In those moments, we know

The deep mystery of our oneness.

A separate self
Is the last illusion to break free from,
The last nightmare to wake up from,
The last sweet memory to let go of.

Break free, wake up, Let go.

This Killin' Thing

Strange and tragic —
This killin' thing;
Talkin' 'bout Lincoln,
Kennedy and King.
Don't understand
Such odd behavior,
Why we always
Crucify our savior.

We crucified Jesus —
Not once but twice;
First his body,
Then his advice.
He talked of love
And helping the lame;
We hate and kill —
All in his name.

Star Dust

It is what it is.
You are what you are
Magical dust
That fell from a star.

We all suffer,
Some horribly and some repeatedly,
But not forever.

Things come to pass,
Not to stay.
Time brings forth,
And time takes away.

Be happy – don't worry.
It'll all work out.
What needs to be,
Will come about.

Be patient with yourself,
Don't beat yourself up.
We suck from a breast
Before we drink from a cup.

Accept where you are,
Trust where you'll be.
Open your eyes and
Embrace what you see.

Time is your healer.

Time's on your side.
The body fades,
But the Universe abides.

I am the Universe,
And so are you.
You are me
And I am you.

Birth is separation.
Death is reunion.
The good life is a life
Of growing communion.

It's all good, my friend,
So enjoy life – be free;
But the kinder you are
The happier you'll be.

Follow the spirit,
Not the letter.
We all do best
When we all do better.

Enjoy your life,
Follow your bliss,
But the more you share,
The less you'll miss.

Be grateful and enjoy
The life you are given;
But remember that sharing
Is the pathway to heaven.

We don't yet know
How to love as we should,
But the journey has begun,
And the ending is good.

Selfishness and greed
Will run their course,
But love is evolution's
Tour de force.

Even if you're selfish,
It'll still be alright.
The fate of the universe
Is not yours to write.
You just won't sleep
As peaceful tonight.

Me

I want to be happy,
I want to be free!
But guess what my friend,
It's not about me.

I want to please God,
So God will please me,
But that doesn't work,
'Cause it's not about me.

Enough about me –
Let's talk about thee:
What do you
Think about me?

I'm willing to die
With Christ you see,
As long as Christ
Will die for me.

I'll gladly give
To God and thee,
As long as God
Gives back to me.

Oh sweet Jesus,
Hear my plea:
How can I be free
From me?

"You want to be happy?
You want to be free?
Let desires for both
Die with Me."

Meditation Mantra

It just is...
nothing to analyze,
nothing to argue about,
nothing to figure out,
nothing to fight or kill for.
It just is.

It's okay...
nothing to regret,
nothing to run from,
nothing to be bitter about,
nothing to worry about,
nothing to stay awake at night for,
Or waste another day for.
It's okay.

Just let go...
of the past,
of the future,
of the pain,
of all the things you can't control –
which is most things.
Just let go.

And just be...
engage the world around you,
love the people near you,
smile,
lose yourself...
in the music, the mystery and the magic.
Just be.

The Poor

We go to church on Sunday,
Hear scripture and break bread;
We've made our weekly sacrifice,
But the hungry still aren't fed.

We drive to work on Monday
And wonder how we cope;
We work all day and earn our pay,
But the poor still have no hope.

We bathe and dress on Tuesday,
Choose from browns and blues;
While children all around the world
Have no soap or shoes.

We use our ATM on Wednesday,
And hope we have enough.
Then pray for all the homeless
Who haven't any stuff.

We call our mom on Thursday
To make sure she's Ok,
But can only talk a minute –
We've such a busy day.

We talk to friends on Friday –
Make plans for Friday night.
Drink some beer and close our ears
To those who daily fight
Just to stay alive
And keep their children safe,

From gangs, drugs and violence
And politicians on the take.

We watch the game on Saturday –
Cheering with the crowd;
Not seeing all the lonely
Who bear a silence just as loud.

"Feed the hungry, help the poor,
Let the rich beware";
Give the needy something more
Than pennies and a prayer.

We go to church on Sunday,
Hear scripture and break bread;
We've made our weekly sacrifice,
But the hungry still aren't fed.

Letting Go

Why is it so hard to let go?
To let go completely of
All we have,
All we are,
Memories,
Desires,
Our very existence.

Why do we fear death?
The final and ultimate letting go.
Maybe we shouldn't.
Try it.

Close your eyes.
Let go
Of everything.
Your dreams,
Your desires,
Memories,
Loved ones,
Hopes,
Fears,
Awareness itself.
Go to sleep,
Let yourself die.
Let go of the person letting go.

Let go, let go, let go, let go, let go...
Peace,
Freedom,
Bliss.

No desires,
No fears,
No drives,
Nothing.

Everything.
That which lets everything be.
One thing
Expressing itself in a trillion ways.
Always was.
Always will be.
Rest for awhile.

Then return.
Hold on again,
But ever so lightly.

Does this diminish love?
Not at all.
It only diminishes the ego
That holds on so tightly.

One Thing

One thing
Always changing.
One thing
With a trillion faces.
You are that.

The atoms that form you
Will form another you,
And then another,
And another.

The current you is not the first you.
Do you remember an earlier you?
Does a later you remember you?
Does a loved one, no longer there,
Remember you?
Maybe.
Sometimes.

The Universe is playing
A game of hide and seek
With itself.

Enjoy the game.
Adore all the faces.
But don't take yours too seriously,
Or hold on to tightly.

Practice letting go
Imagine past and future faces.

Or climb to the top,
And just enjoy
Watching the children play.

Incarnations

Humans need God to be incarnate,
The spirit to become flesh,
Energy to become matter,

Saint John expressed it well when he assured his flock,
"That which was from the beginning...we have heard...
We have seen with our eyes...our hands have touched."

Humans need to hear, see and touch God.

Humans need
God to have a human face,

Be it Jesus, Buddha, Krishna or Mohammed.

Humans need stories, statues and sacred spaces
To assure them of God's presence.

Protestants need Bibles, buildings and beliefs.
Catholics need the Eucharist, popes and priests.

Not a problem,
Until we become smaller than we are,
Allowing our local incarnations and icons
To define
The infinite complexities and mysteries of What Is.

Then we need an enemy to defeat,
And blame
And punish,
Subconsciously soothing our own guilt,
And convincing ourselves that our god is the true one.

As a wise man once said,
"The god that can be named is not God."
Even the Jews, who knew God's name,
Would not dare speak it,
Or fully write it,
Or make an image;
Leaving us wondering how to pronounce YHWH.

Do we really need special incarnations?
Is not everything an incarnation of God?
Saint Paul wrote about a time when "God will be all in all".
He is and always was –
We just forgot.

Is not heaven Her throne and the earth Her footstool?
Did not Jesus say, "You all are Gods"?
Did not Saint Paul also write, "Since the creation of the world
God's invisible qualities have been clearly seen and
understood
From what has been made"

Let nature be your scripture,
The universe your temple,
The earth your sacred space,
Creatures of land, air and water your saints,
The sounds of nature your hymns,
Rivers, mountains, forests and seas your icons,
The seasons your liturgical calendar.
See the face of God shining through all people,
Especially your children.

The greatest miracle is you,
And me,
And the world around us.

What more do we need?

Thank You Universe

Born poor
Yet smart enough to play the game,
And often win.
Shot in Dallas,
Embarrassed and exploited;
Yet loved and protected.

Overwhelmed by more death,
Suddenly and often.
I grew up.
And perhaps grew old prematurely.

Swallowed up by a system
That brainwashes millions,
No, billions.
Wasted years? Hard to say.
So many good people
Many of whom became family,
At least for awhile.

The system taught me to work hard
And sacrifice
And think deeply,
Ultimately, more deeply than they intended.
I asked big questions
And found a few big answers.

Would not be here,
Had I not been shot there.
May not have met my soul mate,
Or fathered four amazing children,

Or been blessed by perfect grandchildren.
I wouldn't change a thing.

My children struggle at times,
Yet they amaze me
With their strength,
Wisdom,
And love.

I worry about the world
We are leaving to our grandchildren,
Yet I trust evolution –
God's greatest idea.
The power of evolution
And the mystery of synchronicity
Give me hope.

I feel so damn lucky and undeserving.
Why me?
No, I wouldn't change a thing.
Thank you Universe!

Relativity

When you move faster than me,
You don't see what I see.
What you see before
Comes afterwards for me,
Cause and effect
Must no longer be.
It just is.

Creating Reality

Like children connecting dots
In a coloring book,
We create patterns,
Both beautiful and tragic,
From a universe
Of infinite potentiality.

At 4 Years Old

The 4 year old I used to know,
His cells no longer live.
The stuff within his cells
To other cells now give.

But still I know him
As myself;
He continues to abide
In memories
And imagination
Always by my side.

Is he less real today
Than I will be tomorrow?
Less real than my brother's ghost
Who abides within my sorrow?
Less real than all my children
Who outside my brain live not?
I say he lives, as do we all
Secure in Camelot.

Losing One's Life To Save It

All one in a glorious
And blissful plurality of being.

Christians call it Trinity,
But, mistakenly, limit it to three.
Jesus and Buddha included everyone
And everything.

All one in a glorious
And blissful plurality of being.

At birth
We separate for awhile.
We feel insecure,
Afraid, jealous, threatened, lost.

We gradually learn to survive,
Trust,
Forgive,
Love,
Sacrifice.

At least, many of us do,
To a degree,
Occasionally.

But our egos resist.

Being separate and independent
Begins to feel good.
But never completely.
We adjust,
Acquire,
Achieve,
Addict.
Something is missing,
Never enough.

All separate in a sometimes glorious
But blind individuality of being.

Then a crisis.
A broken dream,
A broken heart,
Tragedy,
Or maybe just old age.

We're forced to let go.
Endure the crucifixion.
Forgive,
Accept,
Be grateful,
Trust the Universe,

Let go,
Let go,
Let go.
It's all good.

All one in a glorious
And blissful plurality of being.

Death?
Not sure.
What is death?
A return home.
Peace,
Paradox.
Losing to find.
Dying to live,
Giving to receive,
Dark night of the soul
That wakes up
To a brilliant sunrise.

All one, again, in a glorious
And blissful plurality of being.

Your Body

Listen to your body,
It has a lot to say
As you search for peace and purpose,
And seek a place to lay.

It tells you where you've been
And where you are today,
It knows your destination
And will warn you when you stray.

Islands

We are islands
In a vast sea
Of universal consciousness.

Sometimes the tide comes in,
The sea draws near,
And we connect easily,
To those long gone.

Then the tide goes out,
The sea stays far away,
And we feel alone
And without hope.

We often search for the sea,
Forgetting that it surrounds us.
"In It we live and move and have our being".

Can the islands and the sea be one?
Can that which comprises the islands
Be that which comprises the sea?

Not just the atoms,
But that which dreams,
And imagines
The atoms into existence.

The Moon

The moon waxes...
The moon wanes...
The moon waxes...
The moon wanes...
I am the moon.

At Least For Today

There is nothing to feel guilty about.
There is nothing you have to do.
There is nothing to worry about.
There is nothing to regret.
There is no one to please.

A Father's Love

"What are you afraid of?"
Asked the father to his child.
"There's a monster in my closet!"
The father simply smiled.

"Look, there's nothing there.
I'll stay with you if that helps."
"Oh yes, please, will you daddy?
It's so scary by myself."

"What are you afraid of?"
Asked the father to his child.
"I've never played this game before."
The father nervously smiled.

"You'll do fine, I know you will.
There's nothing there to fear."
"Are you sure, dad? Thanks for coming.
It helps to know you're here."

"What if I mess up today?
I'll look like such a fool."
"You won't, but if you do, that's fine;
I used to mess up, too."

"What are you afraid of?"
Asked the father to his child.
"I've never lived away from home."
The father tried to smile.

"It'll go by fast, and we'll visit soon.

It's really not that far."
"Thanks dad. I feel better now.
Thanks for helping me pack the car."

"What are you afraid of?"
Asked the father to his child.
"I've never gotten married before."
The father forced a smile.

"Why, you two are so in love,
Nothing will spoil this day!"
"Thanks dad, you know I love you, too.
I'm glad you're here today."

"What are you afraid of?"
Asked the father to his child.
"I've never had a child before."
The father proudly smiled.

"Nothing to it. You're a natural.
Just be there – that's the key."
"Oh dad, I'll be there all the time,
Just like you were there for me."

"What are you afraid of?"
Asked The Father to his child.
"I've never had to die before."
The Father graciously smiled.

"Just let go, it'll be Ok.
Close your eyes - just let it be."
"My God, My God, I'm so afraid.
Why hast thou forsaken me?"

"Peace my child. I've been there, too.
Let go and fall toward me."
"I love you more than words can tell.
Let go...let go...be free."

Being

What are you?
I just am.
Where did you come from?
Everywhere
When did you arrive?
I never left.
Where will you go?
I'm already there.
How long will you stay?
Forever.
Who are you?
There's nothing that I'm not.
Why are you?
No reason
I just am.

Body Surfing

I watch the waves slowly rise,
Then peak, crash and fade.
Where do they come from?
Where do they go?
Why am I mesmerized?

They arise out of the great sea
That is always and everywhere.
They return to that same great sea,
Only to rise again,
In another place - another time.
Unique, yet always the same.

A million arms reaching out
From the eternal depths,
Struggling to touch the infinite blue sky,
And finally embrace the truth.
Content to rise and play...
With the surfers, the gulls, the wind.

And me, as I lose myself
In their message
And their mystery,
I wade further and further from the shore
To catch my ride,
I dive forward and let go –
As the wave engulfs me.
I am that wave.

Breathe

Breathe deeply...
The Kingdom of Heaven is within you.
Be still and know God.
Let your whole being become a silent prayer.
Be here now.
Breathe deeply.

Breathe freely...
Naked you came into the world – leave the same way.
The world will try to clothe you – don't let it.
The world will sell you "happiness" – don't buy it.
Sell your possessions – travel lightly - blessed are the poor.
Breathe freely.

Breathe generously...
You're not your brother's keeper; you are your brother... and sister.
Know yourself in the poor and the hungry.
The world holds on tightly – let go.
Lose yourself in all that is not self.
Make love to all that lives.
Breathe generously.

Breathe naturally...
Follow your bliss.
Do the one thing you were born to do.
The world will give you a name – reject it.
Follow the narrow path; enter by the narrow gate.
Breathe naturally.

Breathe fearlessly...
Fear not your final breath.
The world fears what it doesn't know.
In your final breath
You will know fully and be fully known.
Breathe fearlessly.

Evolution

I watch the world around me
And anger fills my soul.
We're all so blind and selfish,
So little do we know.
I blame the politicians,
And then I blame the preachers.
Then I blame us all –
We're such ignorant little creatures.

But then I see the bigger picture –
Today is just today.
Tomorrow will be much better
As evolution finds its way
Into a world much wiser,
More loving and less greedy.
A world where those who have the most,
Share with those more needy.

Is there such a purpose,
Is there such a goal?
Does my quest for justice
Reveal it in my soul?
When I try to change your mind
And fill you with compassion,
Is it just my ego,
Or is there a deeper passion
That goes beyond my own soul
And strikes the very heart
Of something deep in every star
From the very start?

Everything just is,
Always new but still the same;
Future, past and present
Are just a 4 dimensional game.
It's all about the ride –
Not the destination,
Sorrow, laughter, fear and hope
Are part of all creation.

But is there still a journey
That all of life must take?
A billion different paths
All leading to one fate?
A fate that's full of harmony,
Peace and deep communion?
Does our conscious trek through time
Always end in union?

All things are already,
And everything's okay.
Let it go and be here now;
Stop striving – rest and play.
But ponder this one thought:
Your random life may lead,
With a trillion other souls,
To an ending guaranteed.

Perhaps there is a place,
To which every world evolves:
To finally see that you are me,
With nothing to resolve.
Are you there now? How would you know?
Who has true felicity?

These two words may let you know:
Compassion and simplicity.

Why Are We Here?

Look around.
No exceptions.
We are born,
Fearful and crying.
Finally we die,
In sadness.

The first challenge is birth,
Followed by the peace of a mother's embrace.
The last challenge is death,
Followed by peaceful rest.

In between those two challenges
Are countless more.
A lifelong cycle of
Turmoil,
Followed by peace.
Pain,
Followed by pleasure.

Some challenges are chosen,
Most just happen.
Some are major,
Others are minor.
Some are shared,
Others are met alone.

The same is true
For the moments of peace
That follow.

One thing I know
With absolute certainty.
Today you will seek pleasure.

It may be the pleasure
Of making a sacrifice for someone.
It may be the pleasure
Of surviving cancer.
It may be the pleasure of eating
Or raising a family
Or believing in heaven.

Whatever brings you peace.
That you will seek.

Whatever brings you pain,
That you will resist and seek to overcome.
When challenges arise,
You will seek resolution.

Thus is the nature of life on earth.

Is this endless cycle of pain and pleasure
By design?
Or by accident?
Do we learn something along the way?
Does evolution have a goal?
Do we discover love?

Is there a destination
Or is all about the journey?

I wonder.

Ode to Martha Jean

People hurt you deeply
They seem so mean and cruel.
What makes them cold and blind -
Breaking every rule?

Maybe someone hurt them, too?
Broken, perhaps, at birth?
You'll never know what caused them to
Ignore your human worth.

(Pause) Let it be and let it go.

People let you down
They're too busy, or else too weak.
They say they will, but then they won't.
You're not all they seek.

They meant to keep their promise.
They feel bad that they're not there.
To help you solve your problems,
And bear the burdens you must bear.

(Pause) Let it be and let it go.

People make mistakes.
You've made your share, I guess.
We all make many more
Than we're likely to confess.

If only you could see the future,

How much easier life would be?
But tomorrow's that surreptitious day
You never get to see.

(Pause) Let it be and let it go.

You now feel all alone.
No one seems to care.
God seems far away,
Mom's no longer there.

Your friends are all too busy.
Your children have their own.
No one feels your pain,
And no one hears you moan.

(Pause) Let it be and let it go.

You've had some real bad luck,
And that explains far more
Than most will dare admit,
Even though it's at the core
Of how this world is made,
And how things come to be.
Humans demand control,
But Mother Nature won't agree.

The world is far more random
Than most dare to admit.
God does play dice with the universe,
To Einstein's deep regret.

(Pause) Let it be and let it go.

Let it be and let it go,
It is just what it is.
Although you want them badly,
There are no answers to this quiz.

The future is not yet,
The past you tread no more.
The present is all there is.
Walk in wonder along its shore.

Pretend you just arrived.
Feel your feet upon the sand.
See, hear, smell and taste
This undiscovered land,

Smell the flowers, hear the birds,
Feel the sun and taste the air.
Lose yourself completely
In everything that's there.

Don't take it all so seriously,
Laugh at yourself... and me.
Play the hand that you've been dealt.
It's just a game... you'll see.

Or perhaps it's just a dream,
From which you'll soon wake up.
If you knew that to be true,
Would you worry half as much?

You're much more than the person
Inhabiting this dream.

You're the dreamer of us both.
You're much more than you seem.

Let your small self die,
As Jesus taught you should.
Be one with all that is,
And trust that all is good.

Your old self dies each moment.
Each moment you're born again.
"Do not judge", "Be here now".
Let the present moment be your friend.

Father Time will work his magic,
Let go and you'll be free.
Let go of all that keeps you small.
Let go and let it be.

Let go, let go, let go.
Trust the stars above.
Let go, let go, let go.
What are you frightened of?

The Universe is a friendly place.
You're loved more than you know.
The story has a happy ending.
Let it be and let it go.

Pam

I was meditating.
An image of my sister, Pam,
Suddenly appeared in my head.
She was killed years ago,
At age 20,
In a car accident.
She was looking at me and smiling,
As if to say, "Everything is ok".
She seemed to be about 16 years old.
I had not thought of her at that age
And with that smile
Since her death.
The image was stunningly real.

I had been thinking
About the Buddhist idea
Of no real self.
The idea that our sense of self
Is an illusion -
A series of memories
Held together by a brain
Designed to find patterns in everything -
From constellations to conspiracies -
Imagining "ghosts" that aren't there.

Perhaps Pam and I
Are only mental projections,
Interacting and remembering.
Perhaps we are only dreams
In the mind of some Universal "God-like" Consciousness.

Perhaps God is experiencing all our lives
At the same time.
Perhaps we are both One and Many –
God and 8 billion individuals at the same time.
(The Christian church describes a similar idea
In its doctrine of the Trinity,
In which Jesus is both
An individual human being
And God
Simultaneously.)

But I digress.
Then, as I thought about my relationship with Pam
And all my loved ones,
It occurred to me
How real and meaningful
Those relationships and experiences are,
Regardless of how they came to be,
Regardless of who or what experiences them.

Even if our individual lives dissolve completely
Back into the Universe,
Like a wave dissolving back into the ocean,
Our individual experiences
Are still completely real
And meaningful.
Even if all of us are really God,
And all our relationships
Are just God dancing with God,
Our relationships
Are still perfectly real,
And precious.

I remember myself
At 8, 12, 21, 41 years of age.
But those versions of me no longer exist.
In a sense we die every moment.
The version of me that exists now
Remembers that version, however,
And maintains a sense of continuity with it.

If there is a Universal Consciousness,
Perhaps it will always remember me,
Just like I now remember my younger selves.

If there is a Universal Consciousness,
Perhaps it will always be conscious of me,
In the sense that I will abide forever in its consciousness.
Perhaps this is what Saint Paul meant by
Being "in Christ".
He seemed obsessed with the idea.

If the earlier versions of me
Do still exist -
Perhaps in some higher dimension
In which my past and future selves
Exist simultaneously
In some sort of expanded present -
Then my entire life on earth would continue to exist
Even after I die,
And could possibly be re-experienced
Again and again
In some other timeless reality.

I wonder.

Either way,
Pam said, "Everything is OK."
Somehow, I believe her.

Just Be

Regarding ultimate questions,
There are no answers.
Perhaps the questions are the answer.
So...
Question, explore, debate, imagine, evolve.
Journey with no destination in mind.
Embrace the dualities,
And ponder that which transcends the dualities.

Beyond the dualities
Of darkness and light,
Pleasure and pain,
Good and evil,
Life and death,
There is simply that which is.

No first cause,
No final objective,
No fundamental reason why.
We just are,
So just be
Here
Now.

Ants

Don't take life so seriously.
Our lives
Are like sand castles on the beach
Being washed away with every high tide.

Our individual self is like a wave
Rising from the depths,
Rolling along the surface, then
Returning to the sea from which it came.

But impermanence does not mean insignificance.

As predictably as ants,
We strive daily to experience pleasure and avoid pain.
We build our colonies,
Collect our food,
Protect our queens.

Like ants, the "choices" we seem to make
Are mainly just chemical reactions
To random events,
Occurring deep in our subconscious.
Later,
They enter our conscious awareness
Masquerading as "free will".

But predictability does not mean insignificance.

These temporary and predictable instincts
Drive the evolutionary process,
Allowing our True Self

To become what it is
And always has been.

Collectively, we will learn to love,
We will learn to live simply
And love generously.

We will move beyond
The egotistical illusion
Of an individual self.
We will experience freedom, peace, and bliss.
And no longer fear death.

We will wake up and realize
Today is just one tiny frame
On the reel of an epic 11 dimensional film
Made long ago,
Being played in just 3 dimensions
For our enjoyment,
And education.

We will see beyond our small temporary self
To One Eternal Self -
One True Self.

In one timeless act of amazing grace
Maya will give way to Nirvana.
Earth will become the Kingdom of God.

Growing Old

I hate growing old.
I hate not remembering
The names of people I met last week
Or this morning,
The intriguing idea I read in a book last month
Or last night,
The important task I intended to accomplish today,
The much needed item from Home Depot,
The birth dates and ages of my grandchildren.
Will their names be next?
And so many wonderful memories from a wonderful life.

I hate the lack of energy and tiredness
That shows up almost weekly
Unannounced and seemingly without cause.

I hate the gnawing pains
In my neck, shoulders, hips and knees.
That slow me down
And piqued my interest in vitamins, supplements
And, God forbid, prescription medicine.

I hate the stupid mental mistakes,
That occur when obvious facts are momentarily overlooked.

I hate no longer being abreast
Of the latest trends in fashion, music, cars and sports.
I remember the great quarterbacks from 20 years ago,
But not many playing now.
And even when I do, I forget their names.

I hate the loss of strength, stamina, sharpness and virility.
I hate being on the sidelines and not in the game.

But I love being alive.
And I love my life,
It's all good.
And I'm thankful for it.

The Death of a Loved One

You say "It will be OK."
You say "God is good."
You say, "Believe, trust, have faith."
Hell no!
Better to have never lived
Than to live through this!
What kind of "God" allows such tragedy?
Such loss?
How can anyone talk of love
In a world so full of pain and death?

Cry my friend.
Your pain is real,
Senseless,
And undeserved.
There are no words to erase it.

Time may heal.
I pray
There will come a time
When you remember your loved one
And smile,
When you are grateful
For the brief time you had with them.

I hope you will never lose hope.

We know so little.

We don't know
That there is not a happy ending.
We don't know
That we will not see our loved ones again.
We don't know
So many things about life and death.

What we don't know
Gives us hope.

Cry my friend.
I will cry with you.

Arguing With My Best Friend

Nancy and I argued
As we occasionally do.

After a period of anger, blaming, distance and defensiveness,
I remembered:
All this discomfort is in my head.
It's my ego
Manipulating my emotions and thoughts
To protect itself from a perceived threat.

I began to meditate:
Silently observing my emotions and thoughts.
Not judging them,
Just seeing them for what they were:
Memories of the past
Blinding me to the present.
The present moment is all there really is.
And it's not infrangibly yoked to the past.

I silently recited the prayer of Saint Francis,
Which I often do while meditating.
It reminded me
That deep peace and joy comes from dying to self,
Pardoning,
Giving,
Seeking another's pleasure rather than your own.

I was immediately set free
From the selfish need to win an argument.
I got up, went to Nancy, held her and said "I'm sorry".

She, somewhat surprised by my sudden and radical change of attitude,
Said the same thing.
It was so simple,
Yet took so long.
We had a blissful evening.

We later talked about
How every moment is a new beginning.
We can keep dwelling on the past:
Reviewing,
Analysing,
Judging.

Or
We can let go of it.
Override the ego
And simply enjoy the present moment,
Letting it be the new beginning it always is.

We were glad we let go.

Frustration

"Oh Jerusalem, Jerusalem, city who killed the prophets; how often I wanted to gather you under my wings like a mother hen, but you would not. Behold your house is left desolate."
"I must go to other towns."
He could not do many miracles there because of their lack of faith.
"Get behind me Satan."
"The Spirit is willing, but the flesh is weak."
"Branches that do not bear fruit will be cut off and cast into the fire."

"A time to save, a time to let die; a time to say yes, a time to say no."
The needs of the many often outweigh the needs of the few.
I can't save everyone.
I am not Saint Francis. I am not Jesus.
I have done what is mine to do; you do what is yours to do.

I am Saint Francis. I am Jesus. I am the poor. I am the leper. I am everyone.
Follow your bliss.
The Universe knows what to do.
Follow your heart.

I Am Life

I am one of 300 million Americans,
Most of whom will enjoy the holidays
By over eating and over spending.

I am one of 8 billion earthlings,
Half of whom don't worry
About having enough to eat tomorrow,
Half of whom do.

I am one of trillions of animals,
Most of which struggle daily
For food, water,
And safety from predators.

I am one of a quadrillion visible life forms,
Almost all of which
Are food sources
For other life forms.

I am one of a centilion life forms,
The vast majority of which
Are not visible to the human eye,
Have very brief life spans,
And comprise most of the physical bodies,
Including ours,
Which are visible to the human eye.

I am an infinity of quantum events,

With the potential to form
Every possible universe,
And every possible version,
Of every imaginable person
An infinite number of times.

I am life
In all of it's manifestations;
Ever changing,
Ever evolving,
Everlasting.

Two Worlds

We've got a dance to go to.
I need a new tie.
You need to have your nails done.
I can't wait to see you in your new dress.

They're cutting the power off tomorrow.
I'll call and see if they will let me pay half on Friday.
How are we on groceries?
The kids need shoes.

The Real Jesus

One night I dreamed I was watching
Old black and white TV shows from the 1950s.
The classic game show, "What's My Line" came on.
Suddenly, I was also a panelist.
Gary Moore asked the three men to introduce themselves."
All three repeated, "My name is Jesus."
We began to question them.

Contestant #1 claimed to be the Son of God.
And to be born of a virgin?
Contestant #2 only claimed to be a teacher.

Contestant #3 detailed how he saved us from God's eternal wrath
By taking our place on the cross.
Contestant #2 stated he was simply sharing the world's pain,
Sacrificing his life for a just cause,
And that we should follow his example.

Contestant #3 claimed to have said and done everything
Matthew, Mark, Luke and John wrote.
He explained the contradictions were due to
Our own limited understanding.

Contestant #1 affirmed he had literally risen from the dead
On the third day
And ascended into heaven on the 40th.
He promised he would return someday in the clouds
To rescue his chosen ones.
Contestant #3 added he would establish the Kingdom of God

When he returned.
Contestant #2 reminded us that each Biblical writer
described the resurrection differently.
He said it's impossible to put into words
What actually happened.
He added that the Kingdom of God
Is always and everywhere,
And within everyone.

Contestant #3 displayed an affinity toward Baptists.
While contestant #1 admitted he was partial to
Charismatic Catholics.
Contestant #2 wouldn't say,
But he often reminded me of Bishop Spong,
Or Saint Francis.

Contestant #2 insisted we turn the other cheek
and put our swords away?
Contestant #3 demanded we sell our cloak and buy a sword.
He detailed how we could love our enemies
And slaughter them at the same time.

Contestant #2 argued that the poor were blessed.
Contestant #1 attested it was only the poor in spirit,
And that the Father wants us to be rich and prosperous.

Contestants 1 and 3 reminded us
it was only the rich young ruler that he asked
To sell all his possessions and give the money to the poor.
Contestant #2 countered that Luke remembered him
commanding everyone to do that;
Along with leaving their children and spouses.

Contestant #2 declared persecution to be a blessing?
Contestant #1 insisted we should file a civil suit.

Contestant #2 pleaded that we all seek
a more just and compassionate government.
Contestant #3 argued that compassion should be limited to individuals,
He went on to contend that Social Security
and Medicare should be privatized.

Contestant #2 enumerated numerous negative things
about money and greed.
Contestant #3 accused him of sounding like a socialist.

Contestant #2 avowed we are all gods,
And that's why the term "son of God" should not bother us.
He admitted, however, that he preferred "son of man" or "teacher".
Actually, he didn't seem to care if we got the words right or not.

Contestant #3 described the horrors of "the last days",
And said it would all happen before this generation passed away.
Contestant #2 insisted he was not describing the end of the world,
But rather the impending destruction of Jerusalem
by the Romans almost 2000 years ago.

All three preached about God's love,
Especially his love for sinners.
All 3 told us to forgive everyone, every time,
As they forgave all those who crucified them.

But 1 and 3 also affirmed the reality of hell.
Even while contestant #2 suggested
it would make us more merciful than God.

Contestant #2 said several negative things about religious people.
and seemed to favor foreigners and outcasts.
He wouldn't condemn homosexuals.
And bragged about hanging out with drunks and prostitutes.
He predicted sinners would enter the Kingdom of God
before the righteous.

Contestant #3 assured us we would find God in church,
Especially one that "preached the Bible"
And "believed every word of it".
But then contestant #2 quoted the Old Testament several times
And dared to contradict it.
Contestant #1 declared the Spirit would guide us to all truth.

Finally, the show was almost over
And Gary Moore asked,
"Will the real Jesus please stand up?"
I waited
Anxiously
For what seemed like an eternity.
Then suddenly
I woke up.

A Perfect Moment

Occasionally we have an experience
So wonderful and perfect,
It would be ok if our whole life
Was simply about having
That one experience,
And nothing else.

I had such an experience
A few evenings ago
On a boat with Nancy.
It opened my eyes
To what life may be about.
I'm not sure.
It seems impossible to know.
But it's probably something like this.

Find as much bliss as you can
Amidst all the pain.
Always look for a rose
Among the thorns,
A rainbow
After the storm
And be thankful for it.

Try to share as much as you can.
Try to never be a thorn
Or a storm
In someone else's life.
Rather, try to be their safe harbor,
And help them see the rainbow.

Be happy and be kind.

All the rest is speculation.

Maybe there is a universal consciousness
Flowing through each of us
That loves
And never dies.

Maybe evolution has a goal
That we all benefit from.

Maybe life is like a dream,
And death is simply waking up.

Maybe the world is much more than we know.
Sometimes, I think so.
I hope so.

But if not,
Life is still a wonderful gift
And I am very grateful.

The Music

I dreamed I was dancing with the Divine.
The Divine was always asking me to dance.
We had danced before –
Sometimes I danced well and felt a wonderful bliss.
Other times I was too shy or too busy
Or too angry or too obsessed with something else;
And I didn't dance, or I danced half-heartedly or clumsily.

But this time we danced a long time,
And extremely close.
Like young lovers being intimate for the first time.
And, although I didn't know the name of the song,
It was familiar and perfect for this dance.
We became one with the music –
It was mystical and magical.

The song seemed to change, as we danced –
Slow, fast, old, new, happy, sad, simple, complicated -
But it was always the same song.

The music seemed to come from all directions –
Even from within.
I could hear thousands of instruments –
Strings, horns, drums – some I didn't recognize,
All in perfect pitch and harmony –
Except when they weren't.
But somehow, even the missed notes seemed to fit.

I thought of all the people I had danced with before.
In my mind, I saw many faces...
And then a million faces –

Young, old, friends, enemies, loved ones, strangers,
Some still here, some long gone.

My eyes were always closed.
We seemed to dance for an eternity.

Then suddenly my eyes opened -
I was dancing with you...
And you and you...and everyone...
At the same time.

But where was the divine?
One of you? All of you?
Then I knew.
The Music.

The Singer

Her face was young and eager,
Her voice was smooth and strong.
She sang songs that were new,
And we all sang along.

Her mind was full of dreams,
She seldom sang the blues;
Her eyes were big and bright,
Her pains were mild and few.

Many nights have passed
Since that evening long ago,
When the smoke was gray and thick
And the beer was cheap and cold,
When liquor tasted good
And everything moved slow.

Now the bars contain less smoke,
And different songs are sung,
By voices strong and smooth
With faces bright and young.

The singer I once knew.
Her voice is weak and raspy,
But she sings with all her soul
Still confident and classy.

If she's bothered by the winkles,
She doesn't let it show.
She still loves and sings the songs
She sang so long ago.

An Old Man's Brain

Has second thoughts about keeping old door knobs
And other spare parts
In case they're needed down the road.

Has both a pleasant sense of relief
And some sadness
As he purchases what may be his last car
Or appliance or lawn mower or suit.

Is torn between
Wanting his children to always need him,
But not so much that they suffer when he's gone.

Feels sad not being able to keep up with his children like before –
Experiencing the "generation gap" for the first time,
Knowing the gap will only get wider.

Likes the simplicity, but is still uneasy
About the shrinking distance between short term and long term,
As it relates to health, diet and finances.

No longer questions whether quality is more important than quantity;
Especially when it comes to meals and walks and days.
Even wonders if living forever is all it's cracked up to be.

Fully appreciates the value of traveling light,
And wants to travel now
Before heart disease, stamina, back pain

And cancer prevent it.

Thinks more about the present than the future,
And worries little about the past –
Which seems so long ago.

Grows increasingly grateful and thankful
For opportunities, loved ones, so many good times
And just the chance to have lived.
Understands how it feels to win the lottery –
Because being born is like that.

No longer gets depressed when reading stuff like this.
Everything belongs and feels right –
Even getting old.

Dying

At death I cease to live,
But I never cease to be.
Who I really am
Is far much more than me.

To live life to the fullest,
To be who you're meant to be,
To see God in yourself,
And to see yourself in me.

To see beyond good and bad,
To love without compromise,
Is to know a larger self
That never ever dies.

The Bible

The Bible consists of 66 books
Written in 3 different languages,
Over a period of 1600 years,
By at least 40 different authors.

The idea that every sentence has equal authority,
Or that the Bible contains no errors,
Is a fairly recent idea dating back to the 1960's.

I love the Bible.
It teaches me important truths about life.
I discovered the teachings of Jesus through the Bible.

But if I question certain parts of the Bible
Because they contradict science
Or history
Or the teachings of Jesus
Contained in other parts of the Bible,
That doesn't mean I'm questioning "God" herself.

All it means is
I'm questioning 3rd century bishops
Of the Roman Catholic Church
Who decided which early Christian writings
Would be included in the Bible,
And which ones would be left out.

According to the Bible,
Jesus said, "the Spirit will guide you to all truth" –
Not a particular book produced by the church 300 years later.

And the Bible does not have to be perfect or without error
For the "Spirit" to use it.
Even Saint Paul, who wrote half the New Testament, said,
"All scripture is inspired by God and profitable."
"Profitable" does not mean "perfect and without error".

It seems that many of our political and religious debates
In America
Are not about God or morality anymore.
Rather, they are about a particular interpretation of the Bible
—
Two very different things.

If the Bible is the only path to God or truth,
What did people do before there was a Bible?
Thankfully, God is much bigger than a book
Or a church
Or any human ideas about God.

Secular and Sacred

Today I read
About a girl
Who once sang for the world,
But now sings for God.

When did we start making the distinction?

All the great teachers of humanity
- Buddha, Lao Tzu, Jesus, Francis -
Taught emphatically
That the world is part of God.
And everything in it
Is sacred.

The world is not
A battleground between good and evil,
Where you pick sides.

The world is our home,
A gift from God.
It's where we all learn to sing.

What better way to sing for God
Than to sing for the world?

Imperfection

The world is so unfair.
So hard,
So unpredictable and out of control.
So full of violence and hate,
And sadness.

Along with brother John,
I can imagine a perfect world,
With no heaven and no hell,
With no countries and "no religion, too."

But this world
Is so saturated with imperfection.

My life is riddled with pain,
And unfulfilled dreams.
I'm surrounded by death.
My strength and vitality
Have turned to weakness and old age.

I, too, am saturated with imperfection.

But then I step back.
I see the bigger picture.
There's another side.

The world is so full of beauty and love.
Dreams do come true.
Mercy and grace are everywhere.

I have a best friend.

We work and play,
Rise and fall,
Come and go as we please.
We have each other's back.
We share each other's secrets and sins.

We grow old together.
Our thoughts remain young.
We boldly embrace wrinkles,
Gray hair, diabetes and dementia,
Death in all its degrees.

Yet there are moments,
Many moments,
And they keep coming;
When I look at my best friend
And know I would not change a thing.

The picture is a masterpiece.
The movie wins an Oscar.
The song earns an Emmy.

I gently kiss every wrinkle,
I feel and taste every imperfection,
And for the first time,
I know clearly,
And deeply,
...perfection.

The Preacher

You dress in fine cotton, wool and leather.
You drive a shiny new Volvo.
The pastels in your silk tie
Match your starched shirt
And pleated trousers.

Your fans adore you,
And hang on your every word –
Until the next day,
When they forget every word.
Although they might remember a funny story.

Your congregation needs you.
You justify their judging.
You rationalize their obsession with stuff
And their addiction to money.
You whitewash the dirty fences they keep building.
You become an object for their repressed sexual lust,
And you help them deny the reality of death.

You soften the hard sayings of the one
In whose name you speak.
You disarm him.
To you, he's just a marketing tool,
A valuable mascot for the team,
As you compete with corporations
For a greater share of the local economy.

His crucifixion was an example for others to follow
For awhile -
Until you decided to let him suffer alone,

Become a substitute and a scapegoat.
Surely, it's more profitable
For one to follow the narrow path,
Than for many,
Especially when the many have so much to lose,
And the institution has so much to gain.

Politicians and their donors need you.
You administer anesthesia to the patients
While the surgeons remove their eyes
And souls.

Worshiping almighty and glorious "job creators"
- Blessed be their names –
You help them rig the game.
You help them exploit the poor.
Guaranteeing cheap labor for your factories,
Soldiers for your wars,
Inmates for your prisons,
Debtors for your high interest loans,
Consumers for your junk food
And patients for your over priced healthcare.

Some of you are blind,
Pawns in the system you serve,
Victims of masters long dead,
Yet still enslaving the masses,
Through your convenient ignorance,
And addiction to old traditions
And old books.

Sober up Judas.
Reconcile with the one you betrayed.
Sell your possessions
And give the money to the poor.
Put down your sword
And love your enemies.
Embrace the true prophets
Who are always hated,
And killed.

Remember,
The one who tries to save his life will lose it.

Mother Teresa of Calcutta

A woman came from far away
Speaking words of wisdom.
Her words so sharp and full of light
Challenged my traditions.

She said my "God" was small
And full of contradictions:
A "God of love" who goes to war
And kills without restriction?

An "Almighty God" who saves a few
But loses most his children?
To violence, sickness, death and hell,
Destroying without rebuilding?

"But deep within the scriptures," she said,
"Are glimpses of another God.
A God of grace who loves all things,
Regardless of where they've trod."

I finally saw this bigger God,
Not in her words so smart,
But in her actions, and in her eyes,
And deep within my heart.

Anger

I'm angry and bitter.
I feel this disease deep inside, and always.

I'm angry
At those who are selfish,
Greedy, blind, arrogant,
Hypocritical and mean.

I'm angry at the church,
The politicians,
The rich and powerful.

Why can't I forgive them and move on?
Why can't I pity them,
And show them mercy and grace?
Why is my anger so deep and constant?

I asked the Stars.
They spoke in rhyme:

"The source of your anger is plain as can be,
Close your eyes and let yourself see.
You're not angry at Johnny or Sue;
The object of your anger is you.

You are the one with blood on your hands,
Like Nathan to David, "Thou art the man."

Confess your sins and forgive yourself.
Then anger will have ceased,
And bitterness will have left."

"Unless You Become Like a Little Child"

Sometimes
Children want to grow up too fast.

They try to understand things before their time,
They become impatient,
Frustrated,
Angry
And afraid.

Rather than simply enjoying their childhood,
Trusting their parents
And learning their ABCs.

We are all children
In Life's grand evolutionary scheme.
And we are just beginning the journey.

So be patient,
Enjoy,
Trust,
Learn.

A Modern Translation of Matthew 5:3-12

Blessed are those who have very few material things
To maintain and worry about,
For they have tasted the Kingdom of Heaven.
Blessed are those who have experienced the pain of letting go,
For they will find healing and freedom.
Blessed are those who reject the way of money and power
For they will inherit the earth.
Blessed are those who hunger and thirst
For justice, human rights and peace,
For their dreams will come true.
Blessed are those who show mercy and grace to all,
Refusing to judge and condemn,
For God will never segregate, deport or imprison them.
Blessed are those who only focus on one thing - love,
For they know God.
Blessed are those who unite rather than divide,
Include rather than exclude,
For they are God's children.
Blessed are those who are criticized for all the above,
For they have tasted the Kingdom of Heaven.
Blessed are you when people call you
Dangerous, unpatriotic and a heretic.
Rejoice and be exceedingly glad,
For you are in the same company with
Francis, Gandhi, Martin Luther King, Jr.,
Oscar Romero, a million other saints...and Jesus.

Why I Don't Like Perfect People

They're boring
And impossible to relate to.

Ode to Gary Calvin

You're heavily invested.
For 40 years
You studied, prayed, listened, and learned.
You developed
A theology, a world view, a system
That works for you.

But as years go by
You notice the cracks,
Not often, but occasionally.

For your world to hold together,
You must keep defending a god
Who loses most of his children.

You must keep defending a book
Full of contradictions.
You must keep explaining away errors

In a human book,
Full of truth
And error.

You've mostly given up on the church,
But not the dream.
Even though the dream so often
Became a nightmare.

You believe in grace
And unconditional love.
Yet you exclude millions
Because they won't receive it
On your terms,

You've invested so much.
It's who you are.

To let it go
Would be a type of death,
A supreme sacrifice.

Like the Rich Young Ruler,
You walk away,
Because you have too much
To give up.

Let go my friend.
That Which Cannot Be Named
Or explained,
Can still be trusted.

The world is good.

There's no need to understand it all,
Or convert anyone.

Just be.
You already have
What you seek.
Enjoy it
Right now,
Right here.

Forgive
As you want to be forgiven.
Love
As you want to be loved.
Trust the Universe
And play like a child.

At death
You will leave it all behind anyway.
Leave it now
And find paradise.

Our egos find security
In what's familiar
And comprehensible.

Choose the Mystery instead.

Be brave and foolish
Like Buddha,
Lao Tzu,
Jesus,
And Francis.

My Dilemma

I clearly see
The deep chasm between Jesus,
And the church that uses him
As its mascot.

I clearly see
How the church
Ignores,
Misunderstands,
Exploits,
Betrays,
And crucifies him.
Over and over
And over and over
And over and over
Again and again.

I see the hypocrisy,
The greed,
The selfishness
The evil.

I confront,
I protest,
I reject.

But, alas, I also see
The ones who occasionally
Find peace and healing
In that place,
And from that pastor.

I know those who
Were given hope.
When a child died,
When an addiction became unbearable,
When a world turned upside down.

And I could never
Take that away from them.

So…

Answers are so elusive,
No matter how hard we search,
But does a miracle sometimes happen
In that enigma we call church?

Not the one that judges
And threatens us with hell,
But the one that feeds the hungry
And restores the one that fell.

When a church acts like that
And provides a healing touch,
It gives the world, as did Jesus,
The love it needs so much.

If I Could Travel Back in Time

AD 25.
Nazareth.
A controversial young man named Yeshua.
I would have to learn Aramaic.

I'm sure he would surprise me,
As he always does,
But here's what I expect.

A poor
But enlightened young man.
Who sees clearly in dark places.

A charismatic healer
Whose mere presence has a healing effect.
Not a physician with knowledge and skill,
But a shaman with a gift.

A social activist
Who said, "The poor are with you always",
Not because he thought the poor are lazy,
But because he knew the rich will always exploit them.

A man of mercy and compassion
Because he knows life is a game of poker,
And no one gets to choose the hand they're dealt.

A prophet
Critical of religious institutions,
As most prophets are.
I doubt if he would call himself a "Christian" today

Or belong to a church.
You have to wonder why he only talked about hell to religious people.

A mystic for sure.
A Cabbalist perhaps.
A Buddhist?
Did the story of "3 wise men from the East"
Stem from an encounter with Buddhist missionaries
Who were definitely in and around Nazareth during Yeshua's life time.
The parallels between Yeshua and Buddha are stunning.

A teacher.
I suspect Yeshua would be shocked at the idea
Of God punishing him for our sins.
A God who has to punish the innocent,
Before he can forgive the guilty
Would surely make Yeshua frown.
Yeshua may yet save us,
But only if we follow his teachings.

A ghost?
I personally know two credible people who claim,
During a time of deep personal anguish,
To have seen Yeshua.
Yeshua was not the first or last person
Rumored to have appeared from beyond the grave.
But he's certainly the most controversial.
Are the rumors true?
I would love to go back in time and find out.

The Enemy

Why do the masses need an enemy?
They feel the need to be rescued.
But from what – they have no clue.

Many are glad to enlighten them.
Preachers tell them
"Repent from your sins!"
"Resist the devil!"
"Be saved or burn in hell!"

Politicians tell them
"Take America back from the liberals!"
"Make our country great again!"
"Back to the good ole days!"
(Slavery, Jim Crowe, Cold War,
No Social Security, no Medicare.)

Who are these enemies
Destroying the country?
Mexicans?
Muslims?
The poor?
Gays?
Liberals?
Atheists?
Anyone who doesn't look
Or think like them.

Wake up, my friend!

Your REAL enemies are

Those who assert
That you have enemies,

Those who insist
You are lost,

Those who convince you
That going back
Is better than going forward.

Those who argue
That different and new
Are bad.

Those who blind you
To the beauty all around you,
And the brightness ahead.

Tree of Life

Enlarge your sense of self.
Find yourself in everyone and everything.

Imagine:
You are that child,
You are that woman,
You are that man,
You are that parakeet.
You are that Dachshund.

Children do it naturally.
Be a child.

Buddha,
Along with modern psychology,
Saw the individual self as an illusion.
Jesus did, too, and said,
"Whoever desires to save their life will lose it,
But whoever loses their life will find it."

Letting go of the small self is painful.
A grieving process is unavoidable:
Denial, anger, bargaining, depression, acceptance.

Follow the path of Buddha and Jesus:
Meditation,
Simplicity,
Generosity.

Smile at death.
Death is like a tree losing its leaves in the fall.

New leaves return in the spring.

You are more than an individual leaf.
You are the tree.
No, you are the forest!

Job asked, "If a man dies, will he live again?"
It doesn't matter to those who see clearly now
That everything is one thing,
That every moment is one moment.

Don't let the tree you think you are
Keep you from seeing the forest you really are.

To My Mother

I visited my mom in the nursing home yesterday.
I tried to write done my feelings this morning.

A good mother is always there…
When you wake up scared in the middle of the night.
When lightning strikes and thunder fills the dark room,
When you call in the middle of the day just to talk,
When you need a shirt ironed or a button sewn,
When you come home with a black eye,
Or a broken heart,
Or a broken dream,
When your conscience is tormenting you
Because you told a lie,
Or took something that wasn't yours,
Or lost your temper
Or broke a promise,
When you meet that special person
And bring her by the house to meet
The other special person in your life.

A good mother is always there…
To hold you and say, "Don't be afraid, I've got you,"
"It's almost over."
"Oh, I'm just folding clothes. What are you doing?"
"You look so handsome!"
"You're OK… but I'm going over there right now – no one's going to treat my son that way!"
"I know it feels like the end of the world, but it's not. She doesn't deserve you anyway."
"The main thing is you did your best. You'll get it next time, I promise."

"Everybody makes mistakes. The important thing is you owned up to it,"
"And said you were sorry,"
"And learned from it."
"God forgives you and I forgive you, and I love you very much."
"She's so pretty and so sweet. I like her a lot. Do you like her?"

A good mother is always there.
And even when she realizes she won't always be there,
She'll never admit it because
She doesn't want you to worry about her.
She knows you've got more important things to think about...

Even though you really don't.

Love Is

What is love?
A confusing question.
Stay with me
While I make a suggestion.
Is it dinner for two
By candle light,
A walk on the beach
On a moonlit night?
A fire in the fireplace,
Lying on the floor?
Stay with me
While I think some more.

Is it gentle kisses
On smiling faces,
Passionate sex
In romantic places?
Is it long talks in the car
Driving out of state,
Or those inevitable squabbles
You have with your mate?
Does it have to do with wine,
Movies or flowers,
Sitting at the hospital
For countless hours?
Is it having children,
Feelings of bliss?
Stay with me
While I ponder this.

If there were no dinners

Or walks on the beach,
No lying by the fireplace,
No kisses on the cheek,
No evenings of sex,
No driving for hours,
No wine, no movies,
No freshly cut flowers...
If the children were gone,
If the feelings were blue,
What then? Stay with me,
I'm almost through.

Sunny skies
Or stormy weather,
All that matters
Is we're together.
Love is not
What we have or do,
Love is simply
Me and you.

Leaving Assisi

When I carve from the world
My own private piece of it,
I lose far more than I gain.
I settle for much less than I once had.

I am much less than I was when...
I own a private pool
Rather than share the ocean.

I own a private yard
Rather than share the park.

I own a car
Rather than share the bus.

I own a house
Rather than share an apartment.

I own a TV
Rather than share the movie theater.

I own a private study
Rather than share the public library.

I eat alone
Rather than with friends...or even enemies.

I cling to things
Rather than let them go.

For when I possess nothing,

I possess everything.
Until then, I possess very, very little.

"For poverty is that heavenly virtue by which all earthy and transitory things are trodden under foot, and by which every obstacle is removed from the soul so that it may freely enter into union with the eternal Lord God. It is also the virtue which makes the soul, while still here on earth, converse with the angels in Heaven."
St. Francis of Assisi

Gratitude & Trust

As I ponder all my yesterdays –
Seasons gone before,
The times I had too much,
The times I wanted more;
The places and the people,
Those no more and those still here,
Some long ago and far away,
Others recent and near;
The pleasures that made me happy,
The pain that made me grow,
Ideas I finally understood,
And things I still don't know.

As I ponder all my yesterdays –
Gifts beyond compare,
I'm grateful for them all,
And will shout it everywhere!

As I ponder my tomorrows,
However many there are,
As I strive toward future goals,
And wish upon a star;
As I contemplate the cosmos,
Seeking some connection,
As I search for truth and meaning,
Making peace with imperfection;
As I think about my loved ones,
And their tomorrows, too,
There's still so much to say,
And still so much to do.

Yet this one thing I know,
As all our days entwine.
No life ever lived,
Was blessed as much as mine.

The Big Picture

Our mind tends to see
Everything in parts and pieces.
We tear apart and separate.
So we can analyze and judge.

But beyond all our imagined dualities,
Ultimately, there is just one thing.

Beyond the dualities of darkness and light,
Pleasure and pain,
Cause and effect,
Here and there,
Now and then,
There is simply that which is.

Beyond our billions of small imaginary selves,
There is ultimately just one self.

Ancient mysticism and modern neuroscience tell us:
Your individual sense of self is imaginary.
And arbitrary.

Think about it:
Is your body you?
Is your brain you?
Are your thoughts and memories you?

Is your entire life you?
Or just the present moment?
Or just some final, future moment?

Could everything you know and experience
Be you?

The more you are,
The less reason you have to fear death.
If you are your entire family tree,
You live on through your children.

If you are life itself,
You live on through every form of life
That has existed for billions of years
And will exist for trillions more.

If you are "God" or "Nirvana"
(As Jesus and Buddha suggested)
Then you simply always were,
And always will be.

This doesn't make the individual less valuable
Or the loss of a loved one less painful.
But it may help us see the bigger picture;
And be thankful for whatever role we play.

Our purpose,
Assuming there is one,
May simply be
To experience
And enjoy what is.

Then relax our grip
And return to the Mystery
From which we will emerge
Again and again.

Love, Laugh and Let Go

Both mature spirituality
And modern science
Tell us that **everything really is just one thing.**

If everything is one thing,
It naturally follows that we should **love everything**.
Because we are that.

And it's all good.
It may not always feel good,
But the more clearly we see,
The more confident we can be
That the Universe is a friendly and happy place.

Then, we can **let go** –
Stop worrying,
And start enjoying this wonderful gift of being alive.

It Just Is
So Embrace the Mystery.

It's All One Thing
So Love Everything.

It's All Good
So Don't Be Afraid.

Staring at a Full Moon Over the Ocean at Night with Erwin Schrodinger

Time and space
Are a collapsing wave of Potentiality
Traveling through
An infinite Ocean of potentiality
One Plank moment at a time.

Infinite Potentiality
Collapsing into one particular reality;
And, against unimaginable odds,
Possessing the ability to observe Itself.

We seem to be the observers
Causing the wave to collapse,
Helping determine its future course.
But are we?

It now seems
Our brains only become aware
Of decisions we make,
After they are already made.

Is something else observing and deciding?
Do our individual brains
Simply reflect Another's decisions
Microseconds after they occur,
Like the moon reflects the sun?

Does this other Observer
Exist in our brains,
Or way up ahead,

Drawing us all forward
To some distant Omega point?

Are our brains participating in
The evolution of God herself?

One Universal Observer
Watching the Universe evolve
Through our eyes,
Might explain why
We all experience the same particular space/time,
Rather than each of us
Experiencing our own unique space-time.

Infinite Potentiality
Collapsing into one particular reality.
And manifesting itself
Through a trillion physical forms
Might also explain why ancients,
Who often saw more clearly than us,
Worshiped God in the trees, the rivers, the sun and the moon.

And perhaps all this explains
Why staring at a full moon
Over the ocean at night
Is such a sacred experience.

Healing the Subconscious

In silence
With closed eyes
While breathing slowly...

And with no judgment
Or analysis...

Observe the pain,
Then let it go.

Observe the worry,
Then let it go.

Observe the fear,
Then let it go.

Observe the guilt,
Then let it go.

Observe the anger,
Then let it go.

Observe the stress,
Then let it go.

Observe the sadness,
Then let it go.

Observe the need to understand,
Then let it go.

Observe the desire for stuff
Then let it go.

Now…

Embrace the moment.

Embrace the Oneness of all things.

Then…

Live simply and generously.

Trusting the Universe.

johnalanshope@gmail.com

*"It is what it is. You are what you are
Magical dust that fell from a star."*

Notes

Made in the USA
Charleston, SC
14 December 2016